CELLO
12 HOT SINGLES

Audio arrangements by Peter Deneff

To access audio visit:
www.halleonard.com/mylibrary

Enter Code
1277-4486-9942-7621

ISBN 978-1-5400-5897-3

Visit Hal Leonard Online at
www.halleonard.com

Contact us:
Hal Leonard
7777 West Bluemound Road
Milwaukee, WI 53213
Email: info@halleonard.com

In Europe, contact:
Hal Leonard Europe Limited
42 Wigmore Street
Marylebone, London, W1U 2RN
Email: info@halleonardeurope.com

In Australia, contact:
Hal Leonard Australia Pty. Ltd.
4 Lentara Court
Cheltenham, Victoria, 3192 Australia
Email: info@halleonard.com.au

CONTENTS

BROKEN

CELLO

Words and Music by MITCHELL COLLINS,
CHRISTIAN MEDICE and SAMANTHA DeROSA

THE MIDDLE

CELLO

Words and Music by SARAH AARONS,
MARCUS LOMAX, JORDAN JOHNSON,
ANTON ZASLAVSKI, KYLE TREWARTHA,
MICHAEL TREWARTHA and STEFAN JOHNSON

HAVANA

CELLO

Words and Music by CAMILA CABELLO, LOUIS BELL,
PHARRELL WILLIAMS, ADAM FEENEY, ALI TAMPOSI,
JEFFERY LAMAR WILLIAMS, BRIAN LEE, ANDREW WOTMAN,
BRITTANY HAZZARD and KAAN GUNESBERK

HEAVEN

CELLO

Words and Music by SHY CARTER,
LINDSAY RIMES and MATTHEW McGINN

HIGH HOPES

CELLO

Words and Music by BRENDON URIE,
SAMUEL HOLLANDER, WILLIAM LOBBAN BEAN,
JONAS JEBERG, JACOB SINCLAIR,
JENNY OWEN YOUNGS, ILSEY JUBER,
LAUREN PRITCHARD and TAYLOR PARKS

NATURAL

Cello

Words and Music by DAN REYNOLDS,
WAYNE SERMON, BEN McKEE,
DANIEL PLATZMAN, JUSTIN TRANTOR,
MATTIAS LARSSON and ROBIN FREDRICKSSON

NO PLACE LIKE YOU

Cello

Words and Music by TROY VERGES,
BRETT JAMES and JOSHUA MILLER

SHALLOW
from A STAR IS BORN

Cello

Words and Music by STEFANI GERMANOTTA,
MARK RONSON, ANDREW WYATT
and ANTHONY ROSSOMANDO

SUCKER

CELLO

Words and Music by NICK JONAS,
JOSEPH JONAS, CARL ROSEN,
RYAN TEDDER, LOUIS BELL,
ADAM FEENEY and KEVIN JONAS

SUNFLOWER

from SPIDER-MAN: INTO THE SPIDER-VERSE

Cello

Words and Music by AUSTIN RICHARD POST,
CARL AUSTIN ROSEN, KHALIF BROWN,
CARTER LANG, LOUIS BELL
and BILLY WALSH

YOUNGBLOOD

CELLO

Words and Music by ASHTON IRWIN,
CALUM HOOD, LOUIS BELL,
LUKE HEMMING, ALEXANDRA TAMPOSI
and ANDREW WATT

THANK U, NEXT

CELLO

Words and Music by ARIANA GRANDE,
VICTORIA McCANTS, KIMBERLY KRYSIUK,
TAYLA PARX, TOMMY BROWN,
CHARLES ANDERSON and MICHAEL FOSTER